CLASSICAL COMPOSERS

Johann Sebastian BACH

by Joanne Mattern
with Consultation by John Viscardi,
Executive Director of Classic Lyric Arts
illustrated by Marilena Perilli

Egremont, Massachusetts

Classical Composers has been produced and published by Red Chair Press Books for Young Readers:
Red Chair Press LLC PO Box 333 South Egremont, MA 01258
www.redchairpress.com

 Download a Free Activity Guide on our website.

For more information about Classic Lyric Arts, visit www.classiclyricarts.org.

Names: Mattern, Joanne, 1963- author. | Viscardi, John, consultant. | Perilli, Marilena, illustrator.

Title: Johann Sebastian Bach / by Joanne Mattern, with consultation by John Viscardi, executive director of Classic Lyric Arts ; illustrated by Marilena Perilli.

Description: Egremont, Massachusetts : Red Chair Press, [2025] | Series: Classical composers | Interest age level: 007-010. | Includes bibliographical references and index. | Summary: Johann Sebastian Bach (1685–1750) was a German Baroque composer and musician ... Colorful illustrations plus photographs of meaningful sites and settings connect readers to important points in Bach's history. A timeline and B Sharp sidebars add details to the composer's life story.--Publisher.

Identifiers: ISBN: 978-1-64371-412-7 (LB hardcover) | 978-1-64371-413-4 (paperback) | 978-1-64371-415-8 (S&L ebook) | LCCN: 2024936068

Subjects: LCSH: Bach, Johann Sebastian, 1685-1750--Juvenile literature. | Composers--Germany--Biography--Juvenile literature. | CYAC: Bach, Johann Sebastian, 1685-1750. | Composers--Germany--Biography. | LCGFT: Biographies. | BISAC: JUVENILE NONFICTION / Biography & Autobiography / Music. | JUVENILE NONFICTION / Biography & Autobiography / Performing Arts. | JUVENILE NONFICTION / Music / Classical.

Classification: LCC: ML410.B1 M38 2025 | DDC: 780.92--dc23

Image credits: Cover, pp. 4, 6, 12, 17, 18, 21, 22, 28, 29 ©Shutterstock; p. 4 © Giancarlo Costa / Bridgeman Images; p. 6 © Look and Learn / Bridgeman Images; pp. 12, 16 ©Bridgeman Images; p. 22 © British Library archive/Bridgeman Images; p. 27 © Lebrecht Music Arts/Bridgeman Images.

Illustrations: Marilena Perilli, except p. 7 by Joe LeMonnier

Printed in the United States of America

0425 1P CGF25

Table of Contents

Music All Around

For Johann Sebastian Bach (YO-han seh-BAS-chen BAHK), music was everywhere. The little boy grew up listening to music. Later he **composed** his own music. Bach became one of the most popular composers who ever lived. Millions of people listen to and perform his works today.

B#

B SHARP: Bach has about 8 million monthly listeners on Spotify today; that's 3 million more than Mozart or Chopin.

A Musical Family

Bach was born in Eisenach, Germany on March 31, 1685, the same year that another great composer, Handel, was born. At that time, Germany was made up of many small states. Eisenach was in an area called Thuringia. Like other states, Thuringia was full of music and musicians.

NORWAY
SWEDEN
DENMARK
PRUSSIA
NETHERLANDS
Lübeck
POLISH-LITHUANIAN COMMONWEALTH
BRANDENBURG
Leipzig
Eisenach
SAXONY
Ohrdruf
Arnstadt
SMALL GERMAN STATES
THURINGIA
BOHEMIA
BAVARIA
FRANCE
AUSTRIA
SAVOY
VENICE
OTTOMAN EMPIRE
TUSCANY

Little Johann was born into a musical family. More than 70 of his relatives were musicians. Some wrote music. Some directed **choirs**. Others played music for people all over Germany.

Johann's father, Johann Ambrosius Bach, was a well-known musician in Eisenach. He played music in church. He played at town celebrations. Everyone in Eisenach knew little Johann's father!

B# **B SHARP:** Since his father was known as Johann, most people called Bach by his middle name, Sebastian.

Johann Sebastian's father taught him how to play the violin. Johann learned a lot about music from his father.

Like other boys in town, Johann went to school. He learned Latin, German, and math. He also learned about religion as did most boys in school. Religion would be important all through Johann's life. He wrote many pieces for church services and celebrations.

Moving Away

When Johann Sebastian was nine years old, his mother died. Just a year later, his father died. Johann was very sad. What would he do now?

Johann went to live with his older brother. His brother's name was Johann Christoph. Christoph played the organ in a church in Ohrdruf, Germany. He taught Johann Sebastian how to play the organ and the **harpsichord**.

B# **B SHARP:** Christoph also taught his brother how to repair and tune organs and harpsichords. Bach made extra money doing these jobs.

Johann had a beautiful singing voice. When he was 15, he moved to Lunenburg to go to boarding school. Johann sang in the school choir.

Johann learned a lot in Lunenburg. He learned a lot about singing. He also played instruments in the orchestra and at church.

Bach at Court

In 1703, Bach got a job as a musician in Weimar. He worked for a duke. Bach had many jobs at the duke's **court**. He played the violin and the organ. But he also had to help around the house. Sometimes Bach even had to peel potatoes and clean the kitchen!

Soon after, Bach got a job as the church organist in Arnstadt. The church had just installed a new organ. Bach loved playing it. The people loved the way he played.

The Church in Arnstadt, Thuringia, is now called The Bach Church.

Changing Music

But, Bach soon got into trouble at his new job. Bach was a big fan of a composer named Dietrich Buxtehude (DEED-rik bux-teh-HOO-dah). In 1705, Bach left Arnstadt and walked 450 miles to meet Buxtehude in northern Germany. Buxtehude's music was not like anything Bach had ever heard. Bach wanted to write music like that too.

This time was called the **baroque** period. Art was grand and complicated. So were the palaces where dukes and princes lived. Bach wanted to create grand and fancy music to match the grand lifestyle.

B#

B SHARP: Dietrich Buxtehude is one of the most important composers of the 1600s; he influenced both Bach and Handel.

Bach returned to Arnstadt after five months. He began to play in a new style. His music had instruments playing different **melodies** all at the same time. An instrument might start with a simple tune. Then the tune got fancier and more complicated.

Bach was having a great time writing baroque music. But the people did not like his playing. They said that Bach's music was too confusing. Some even complained that he made "strange sounds."

Johann Goes to Jail

Bach didn't care what people thought. He continued to write and play his fancy, complicated music. During this time, he wrote the *Toccata and Fugue in D Minor.* This music was big and powerful. It even made the church windows shake! You may have heard this music in the background of scary movies.

By 1708, Bach was well-known for his church music. Bach wrote hundreds of **cantatas** for church services. These pieces included **hymns** for people to sing.

In 1708, Bach left his job at Arnstadt. He began working for Duke Wilhelm Ernst. He wrote beautiful music. But Bach thought the duke was too bossy. In 1717, Bach got a new job. This made the duke angry. He threw Bach in jail to keep him from leaving!

Bach stayed in jail for a few weeks. Finally, he was released and went to his new job. There he worked for Prince Leopold. Bach and the prince got along well. While he was there, he wrote *The Well-Tempered Clavier* and *The Little Organ Book*. Students still learn this music today, 300 years after Bach wrote it.

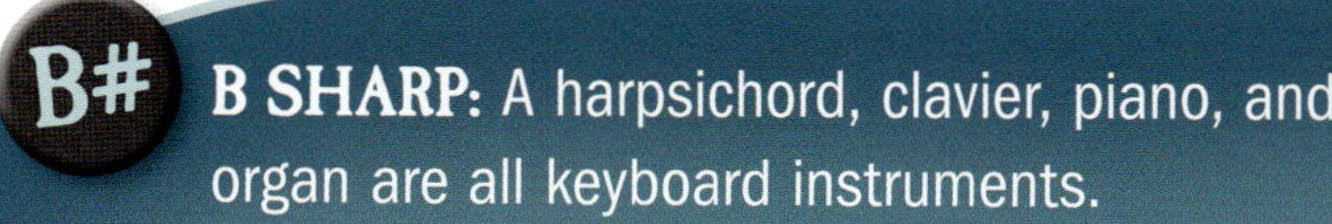

B SHARP: A harpsichord, clavier, piano, and organ are all keyboard instruments.

In 1720, Prince Leopold got married. His new wife did not like music. Prince Leopold then stopped liking music too. He even got rid of the palace orchestra!

Bach knew it was time to get another job. But first, he wrote one of his most famous works. It is called the *Brandenburg Concertos*. The music included **concertos** for different instruments. Bach's new music was happy and lively.

B# **B SHARP:** In 1747, Bach played for Frederick the Great, King of Prussia. Instead of writing music ahead of time, he made up the tunes in front of the king. He was named by the king as Court Composer, a great honor.

The Final Years

In 1723, Bach became the director of music in Leipzig, Germany. He had a lot to do in his new job. Bach wrote music for churches. He directed a school choir. He also composed music for special events in the city.

Johann Sebastian Bach was very happy living in Leipzig. He and his wife Anna Magdalena had 20 children. Bach loved his big family. He made sure they all learned how to play and write music.

Bach died in 1750. He was 65 years old. During his life, he composed some of the world's most beautiful music. His music tells stories. It shares feelings like happiness and sadness. Bach's music thrills listeners today much like it did 300 years ago.

Statue of Johann Sebastian Bach at the St. Thomas Church in Leipzig, Germany.

Important Dates in J. S. Bach's Life

1685 Johann Sebastian Bach is born in Eisenach, Germany, the youngest of 8 children.

1695 After losing both parents, Johann Sebastian Bach lives 5 years with his oldest brother Johann Christoph.

1703 Bach gets his first job at a church in Arnstad.

1704 At about age 19, Bach walks 450 miles to hear and meet composer Dietrich Buxtehude.

1707 Bach marries Maria who dies suddenly in 1720.

1721 Bach marries Anna Magdalena; they were together nearly 30 years.

1750 Bach becomes blind after difficult eye surgery. He dies of a stroke in Leipzig, Germany, later that year.

Wilhelm Friedemann Bach
1710-1784

Carl Philipp Emanuel Bach
1714-1788

Johann Christoph Friedrich Bach
1732-1795

Johann Christian Bach
1735-1782

B SHARP: Bach had 20 children in all with his two wives. Four of Bach's sons (shown here) became famous musicians too.

Glossary

baroque a style popular in the 1600s and 1700s that includes many grand details

cantatas music that features both voices and instruments

choirs groups of people who sing together

composed wrote or created a work of art

concerto A piece of music for one instrument accompanied by an orchestra

court the household of a royal person

harpsichord a keyboard instrument

hymns songs praising God that are often sung in church

melodies series of notes that create a tune

Read More About Bach

du Bouchet, Paule. *Johann Sebastian Bach*. First Discovery Music, 2002.

Leonard, Thomas. *Becoming Bach*. Roaring Brook Press, 2017.

Summerer, Eric. *Johann Sebastian Bach*, Rosen, 2006.

Venezia, Mike. *Johann Sebastian Bach*. Children's Press, 2017.

Index